THIS BOOK BELONGS TO

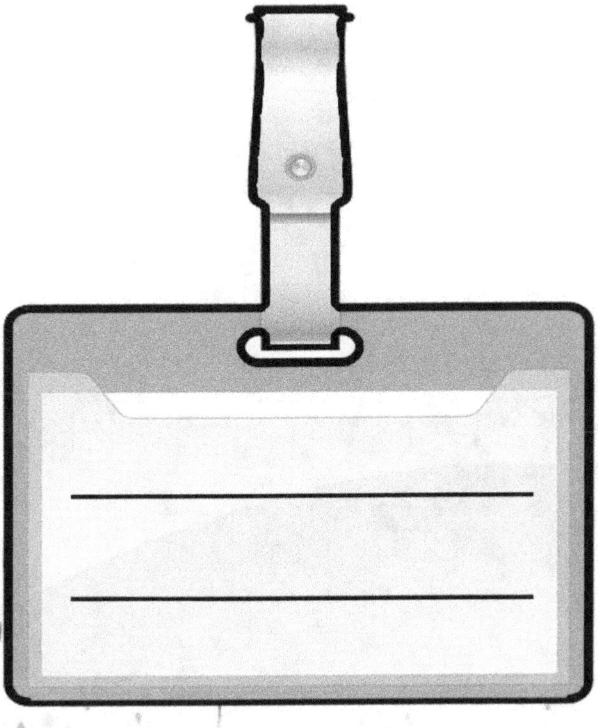

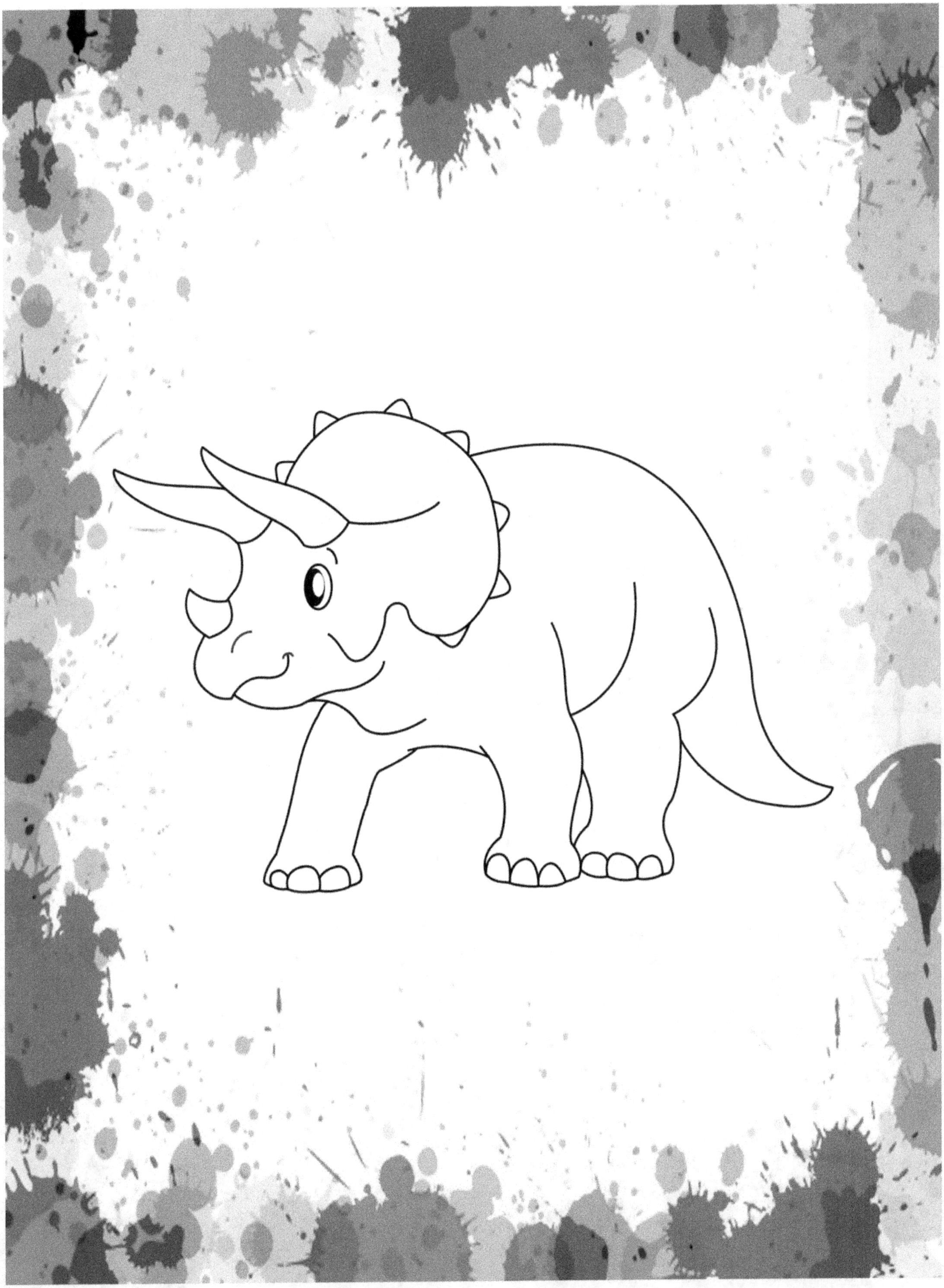

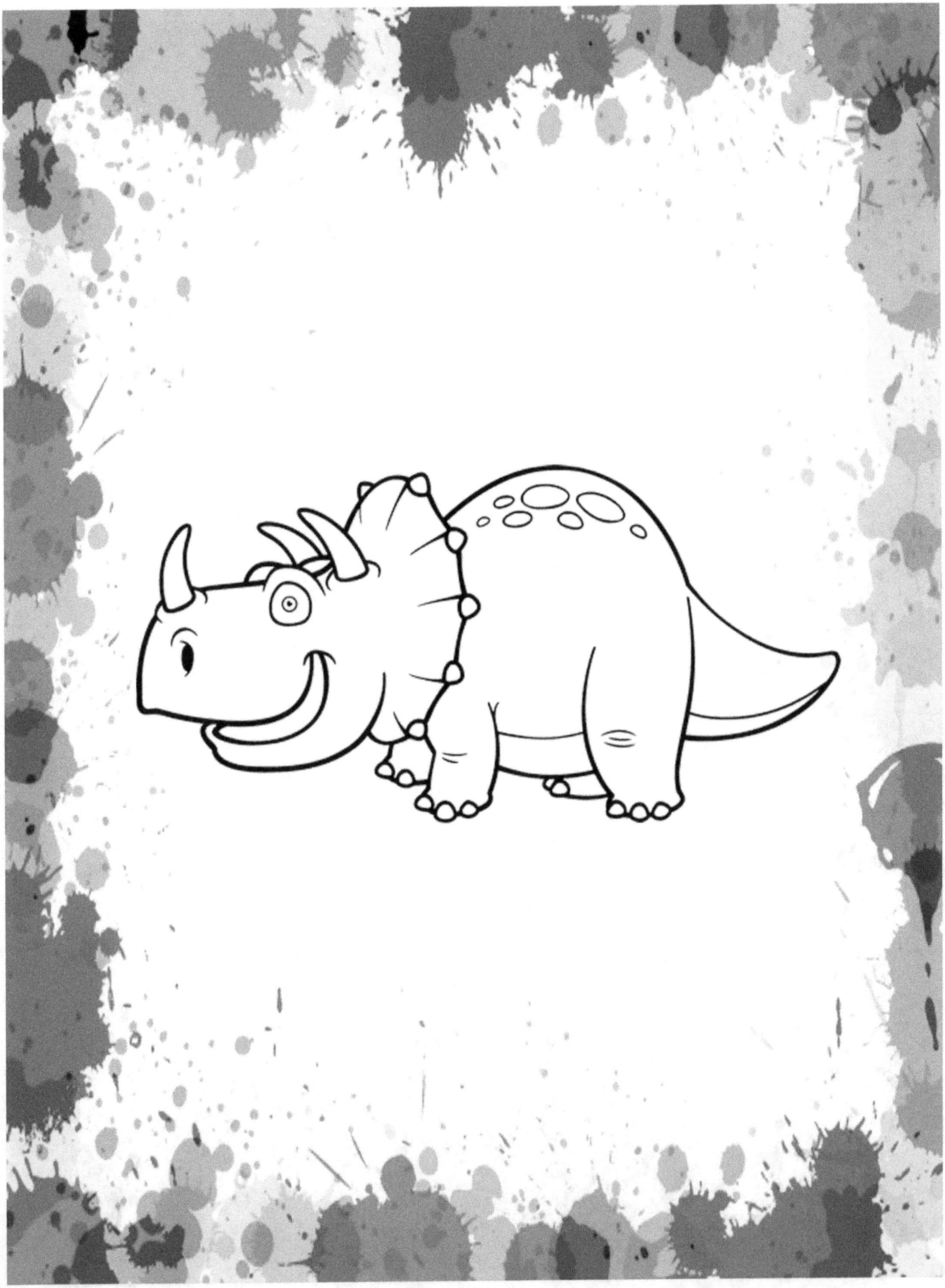

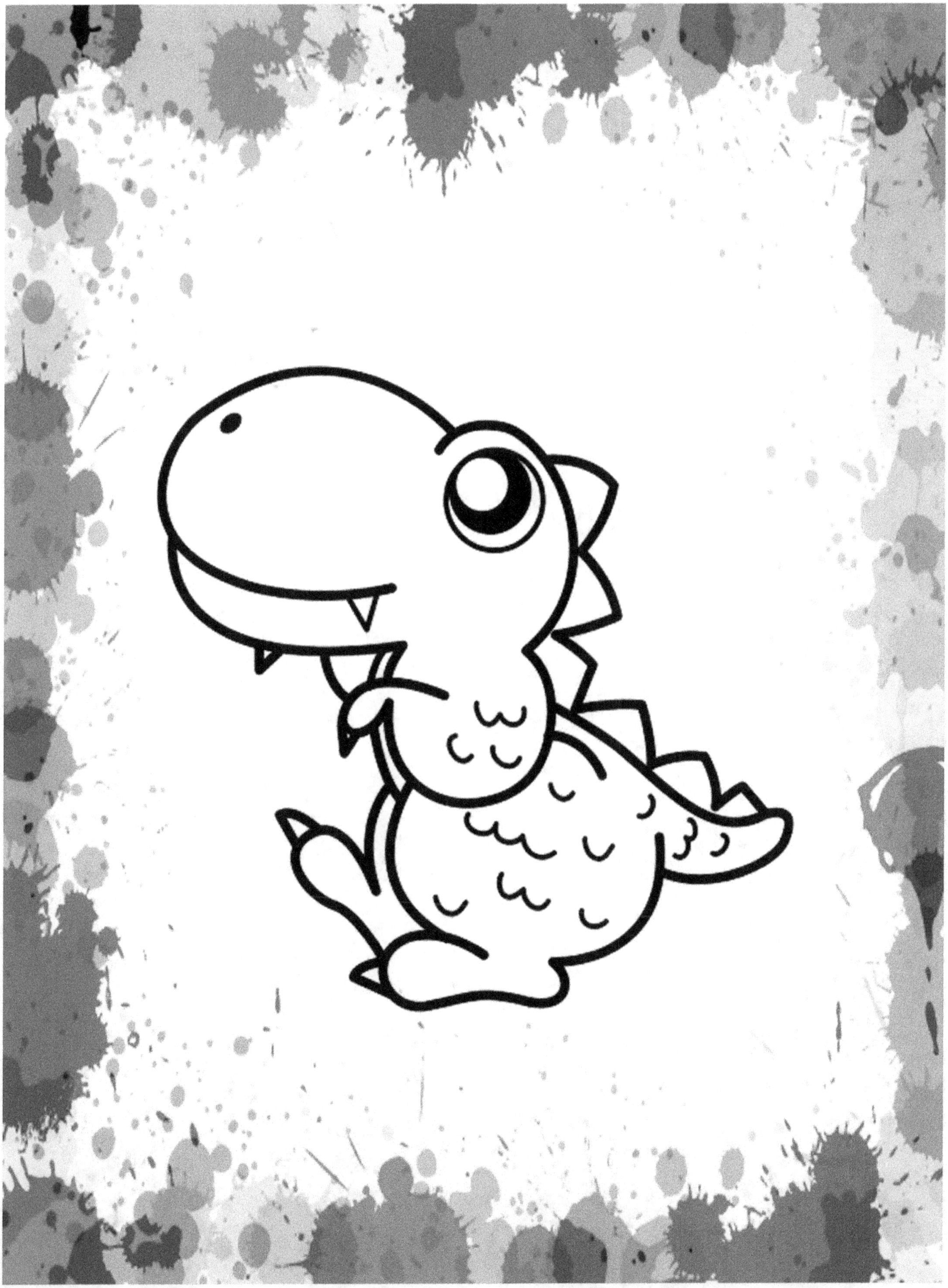

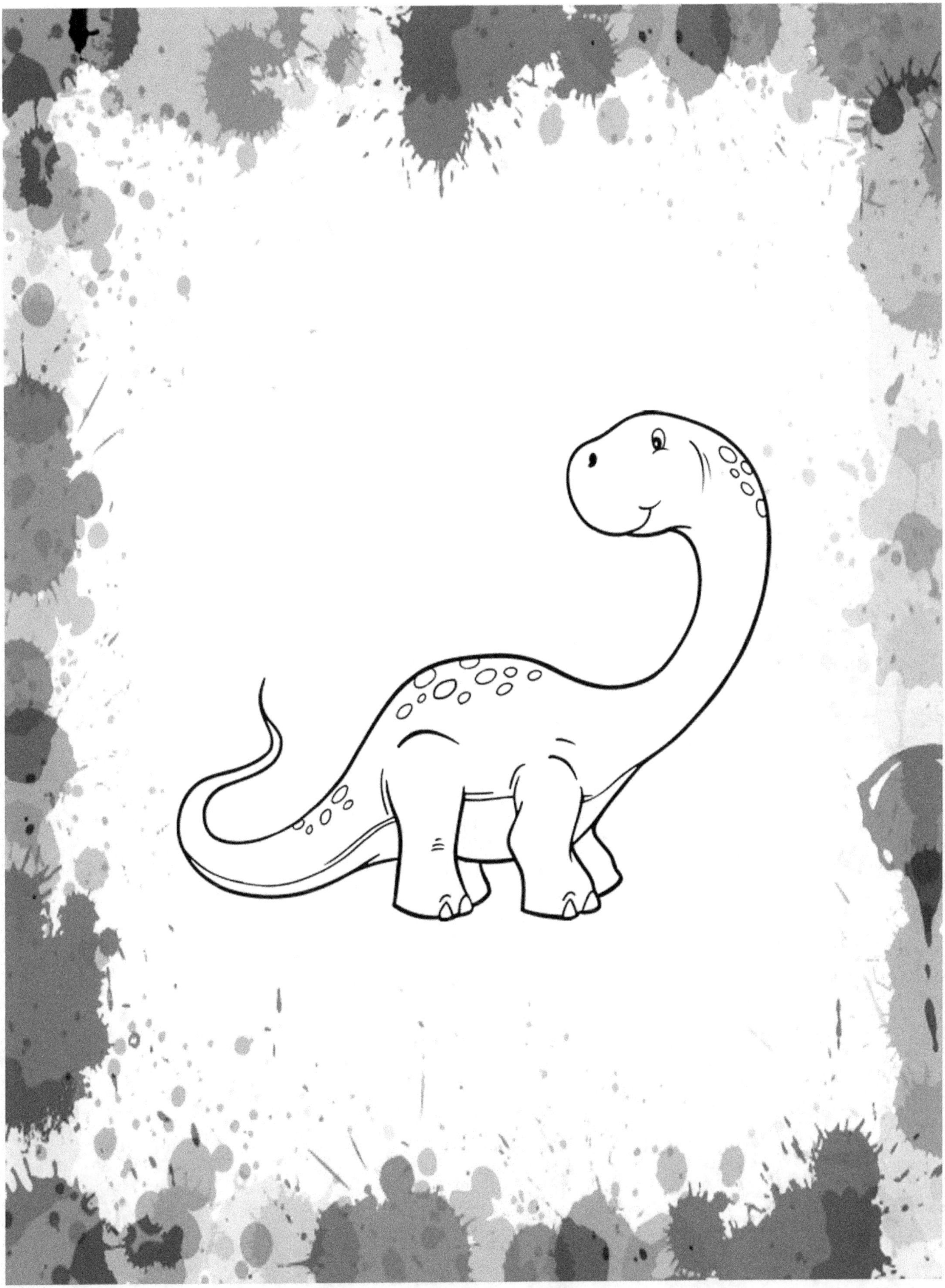

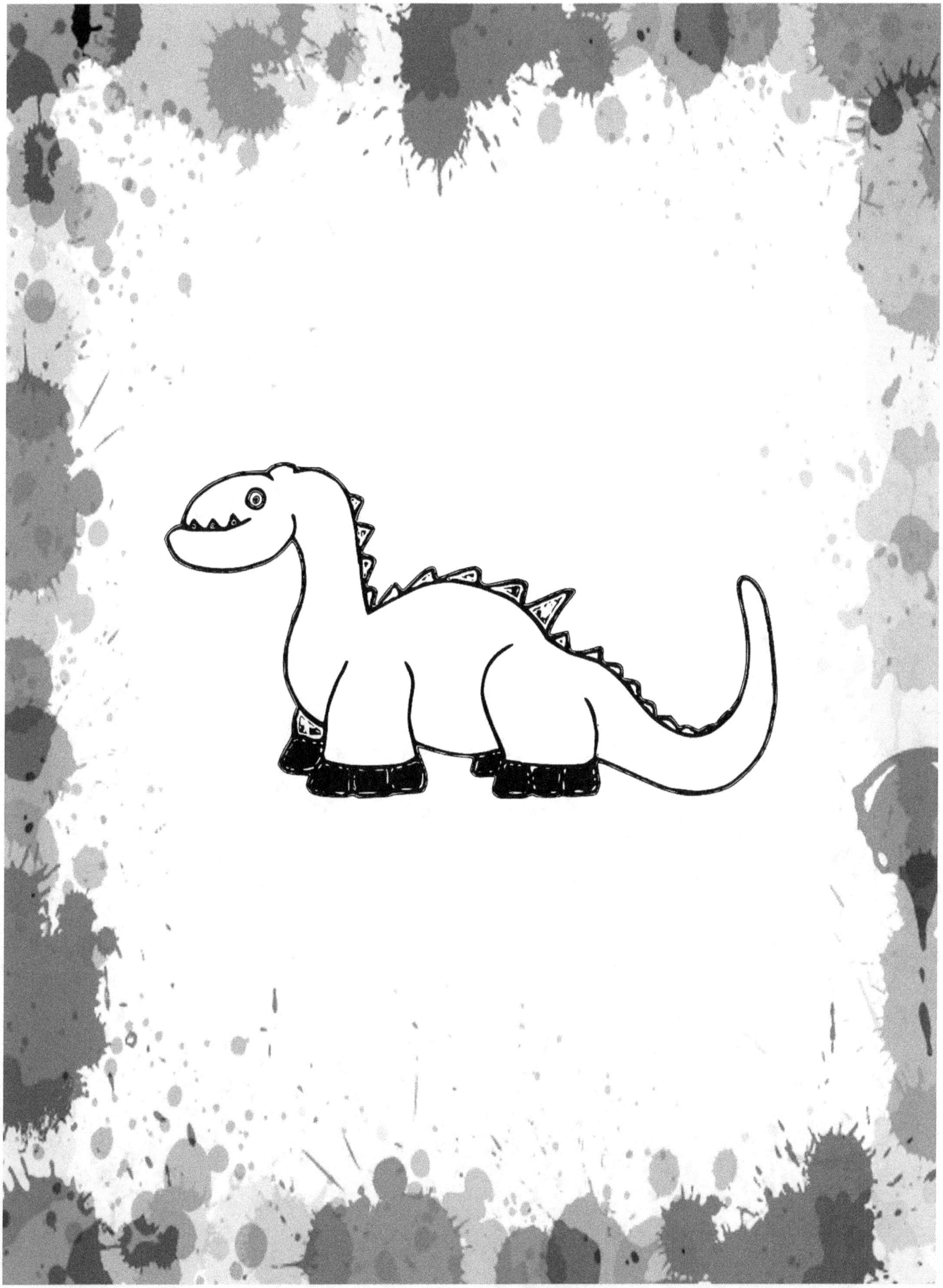

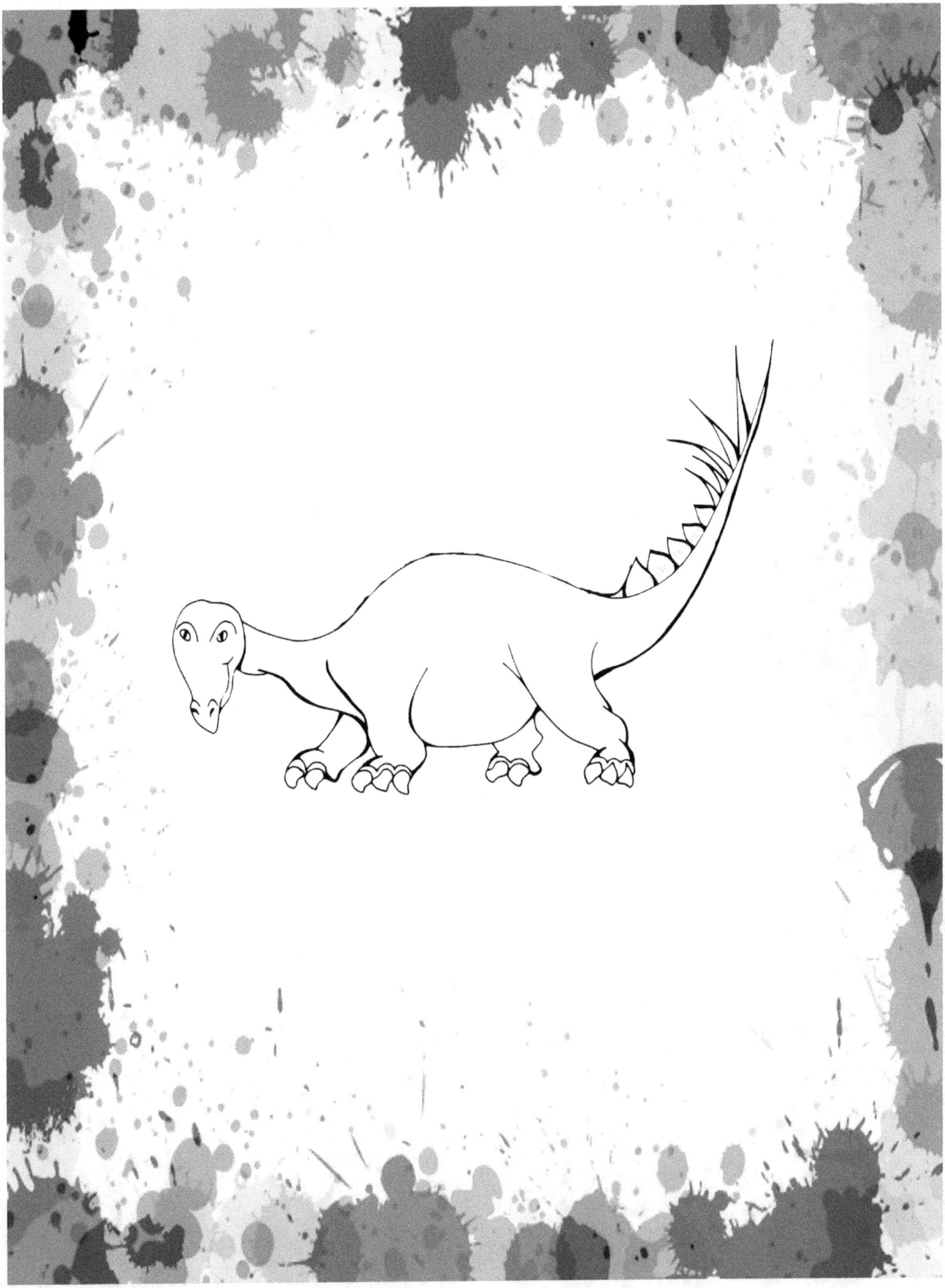

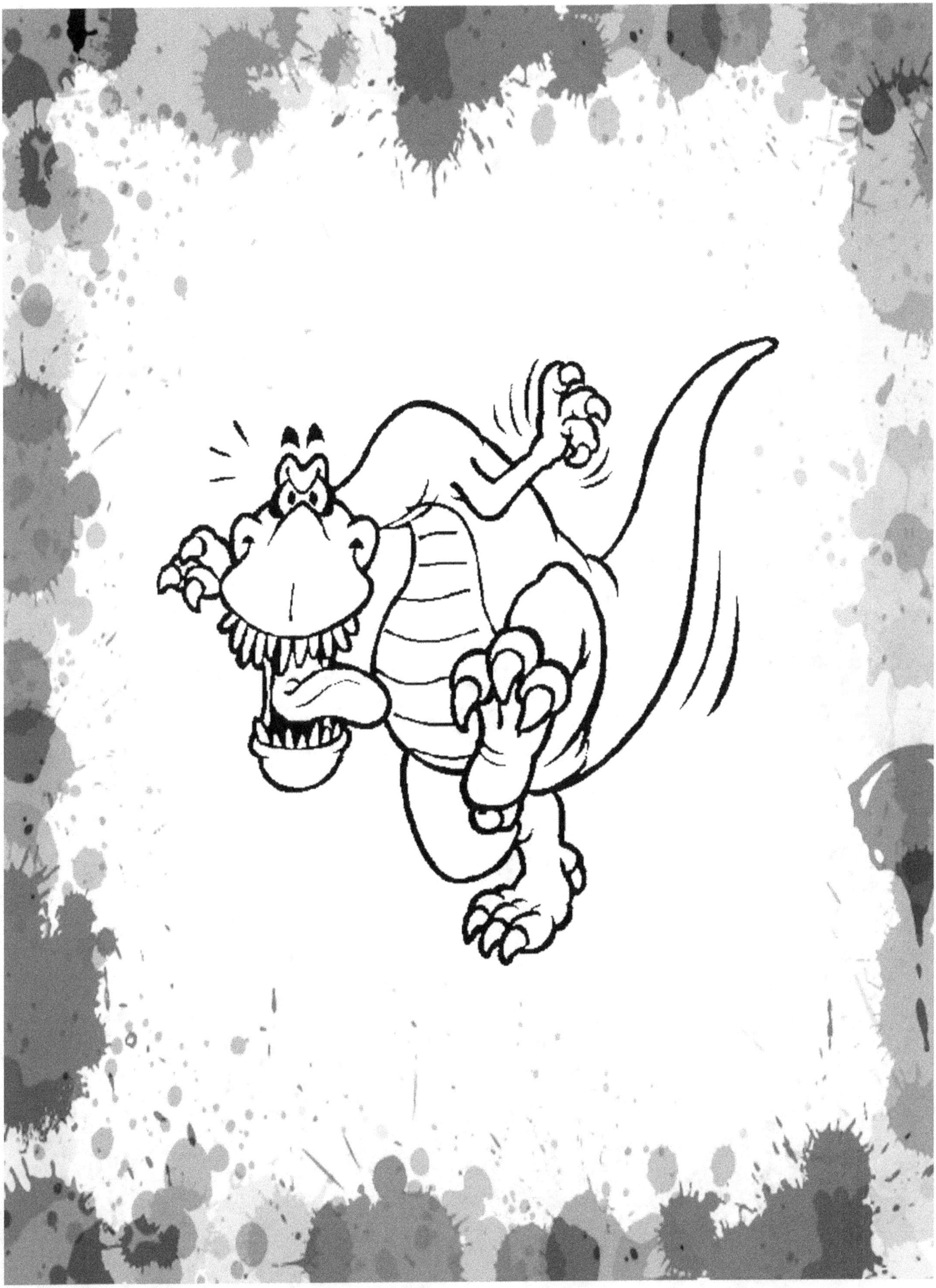

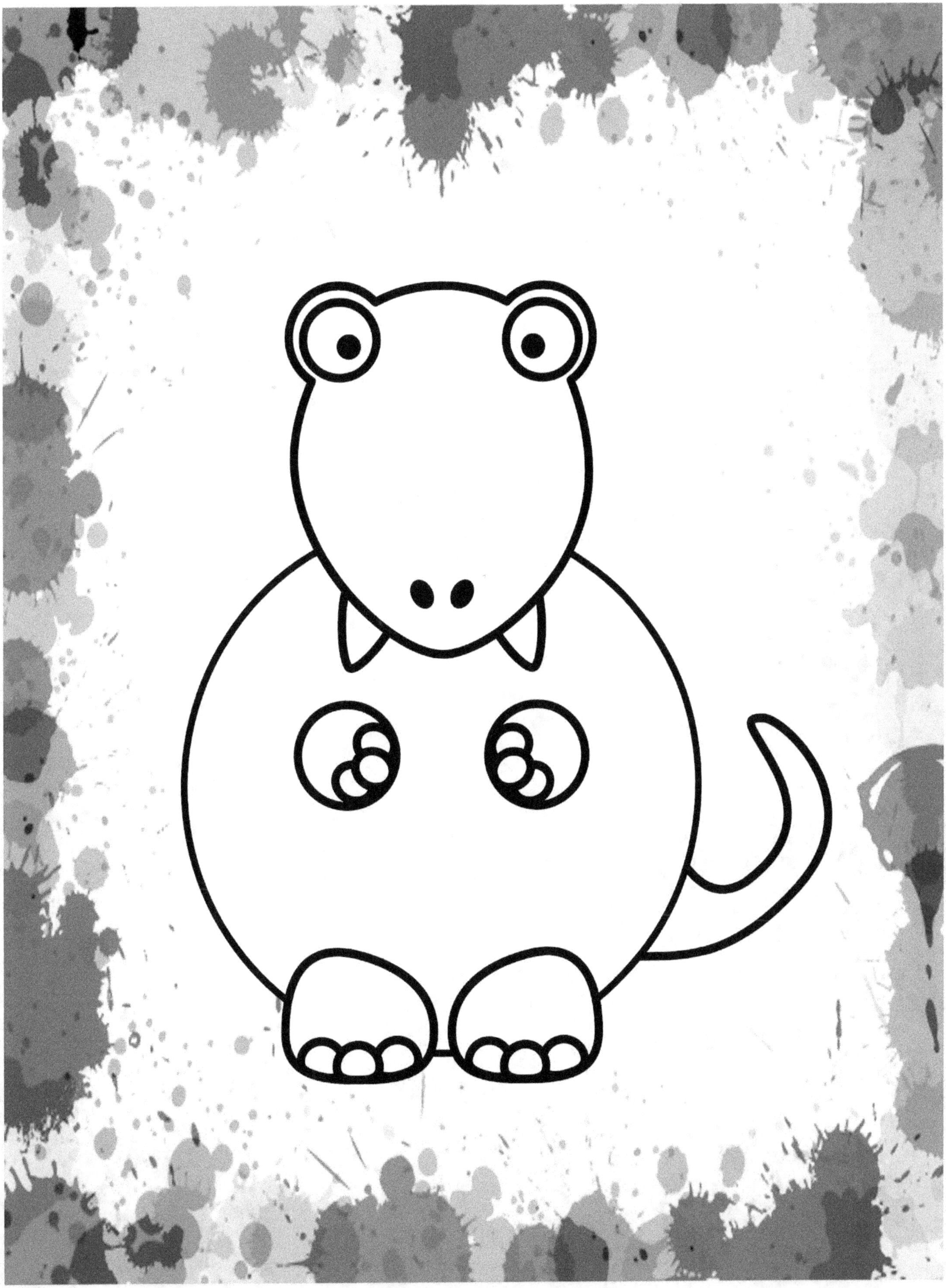

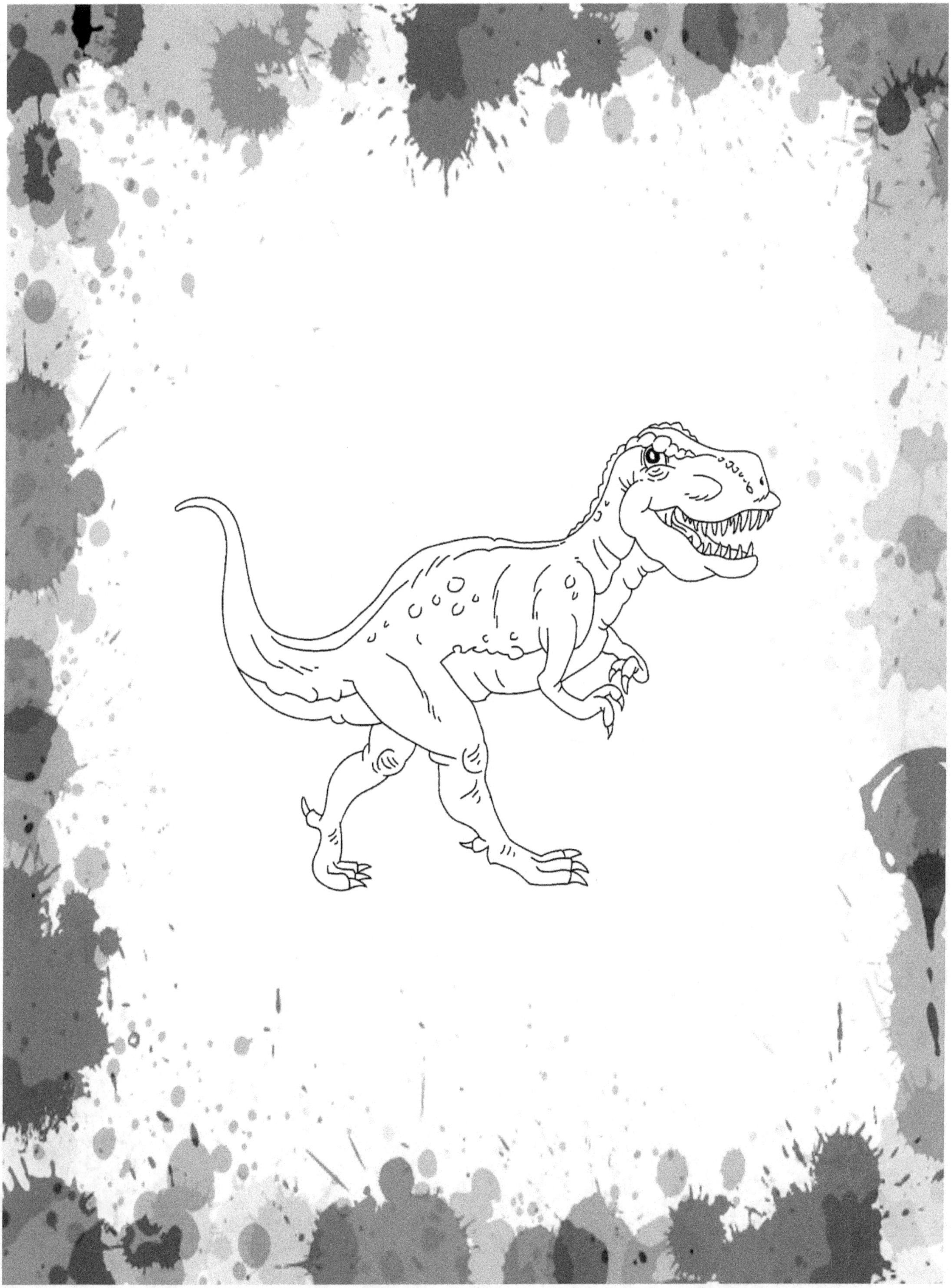

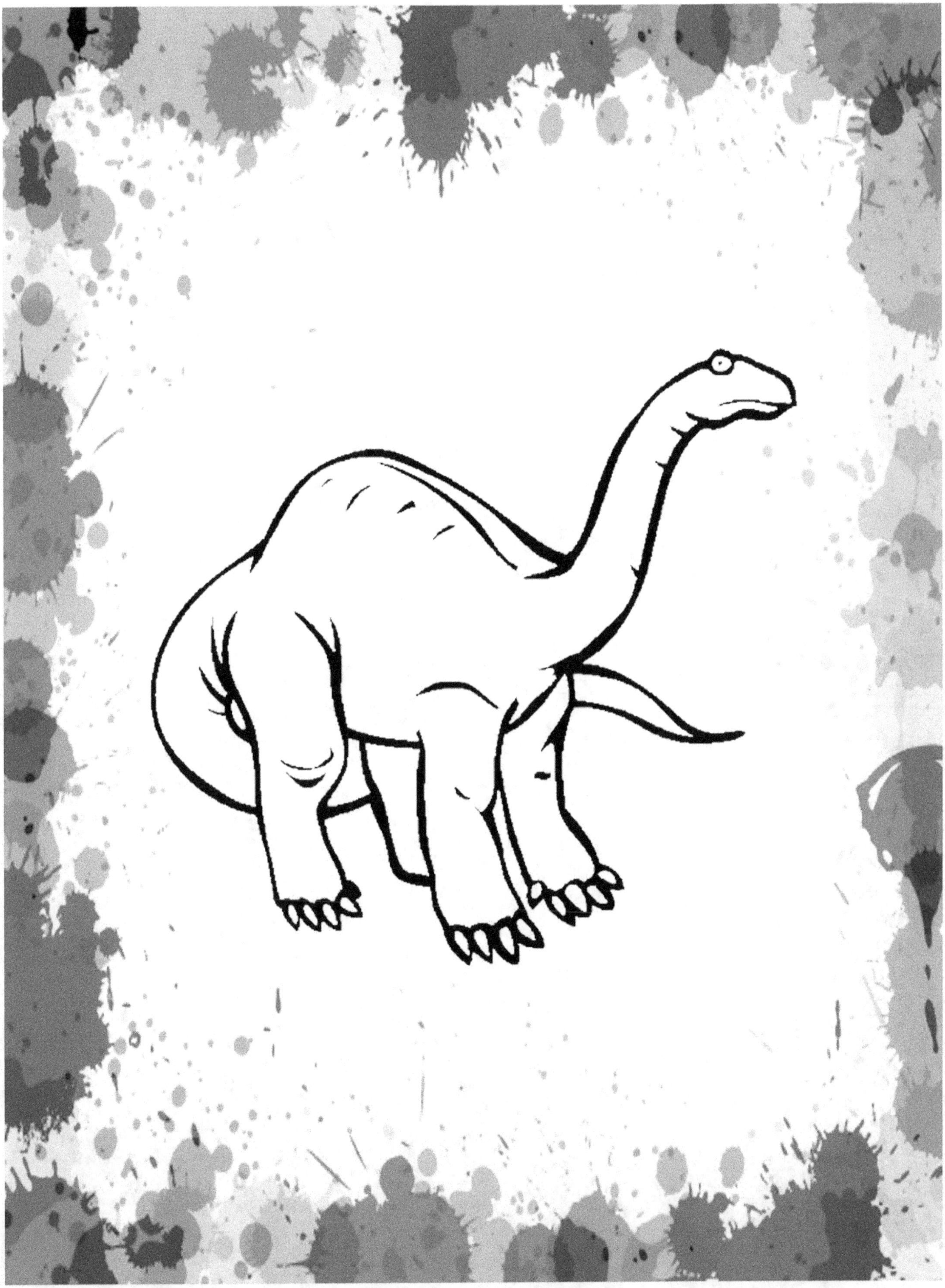

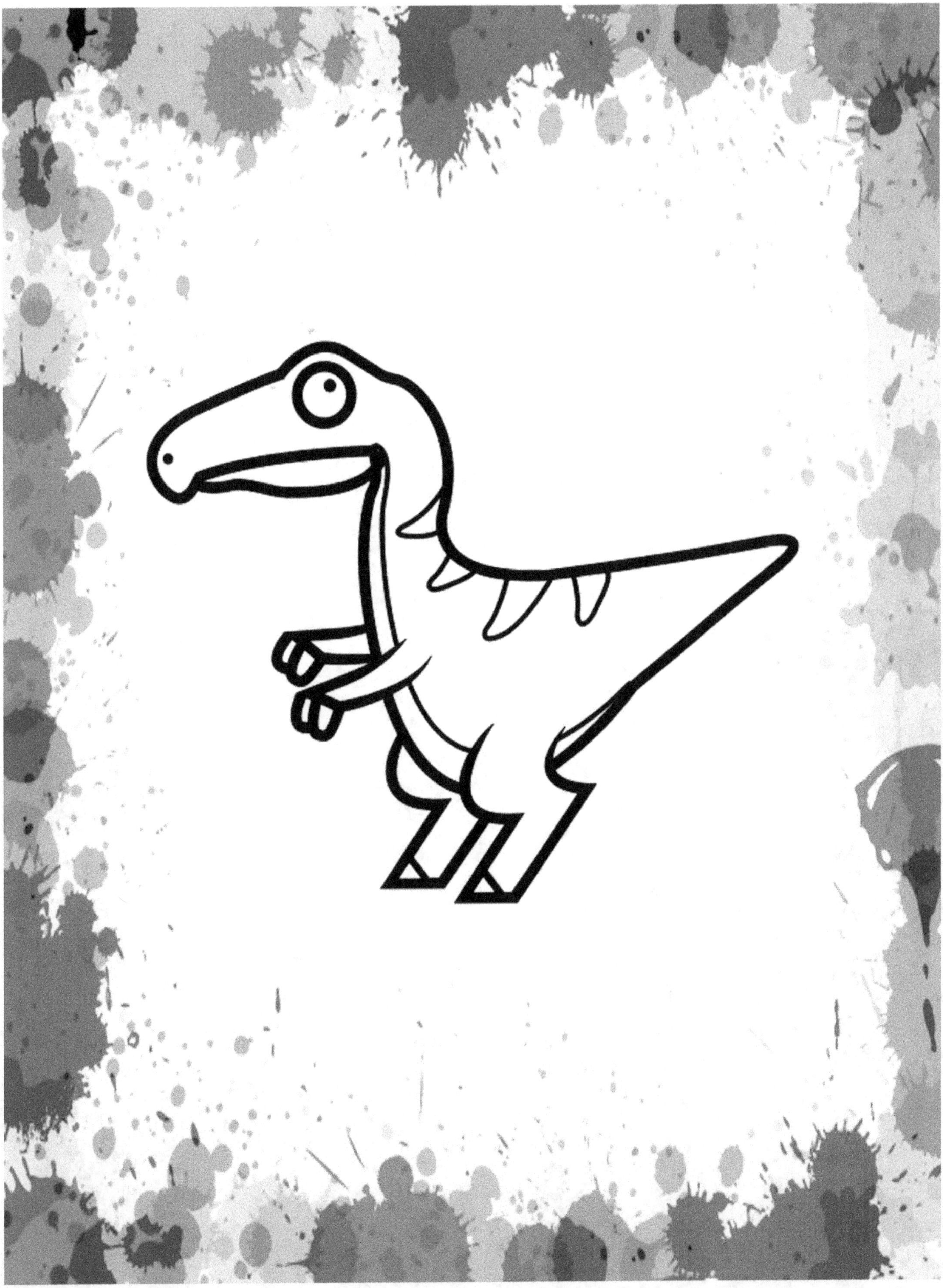

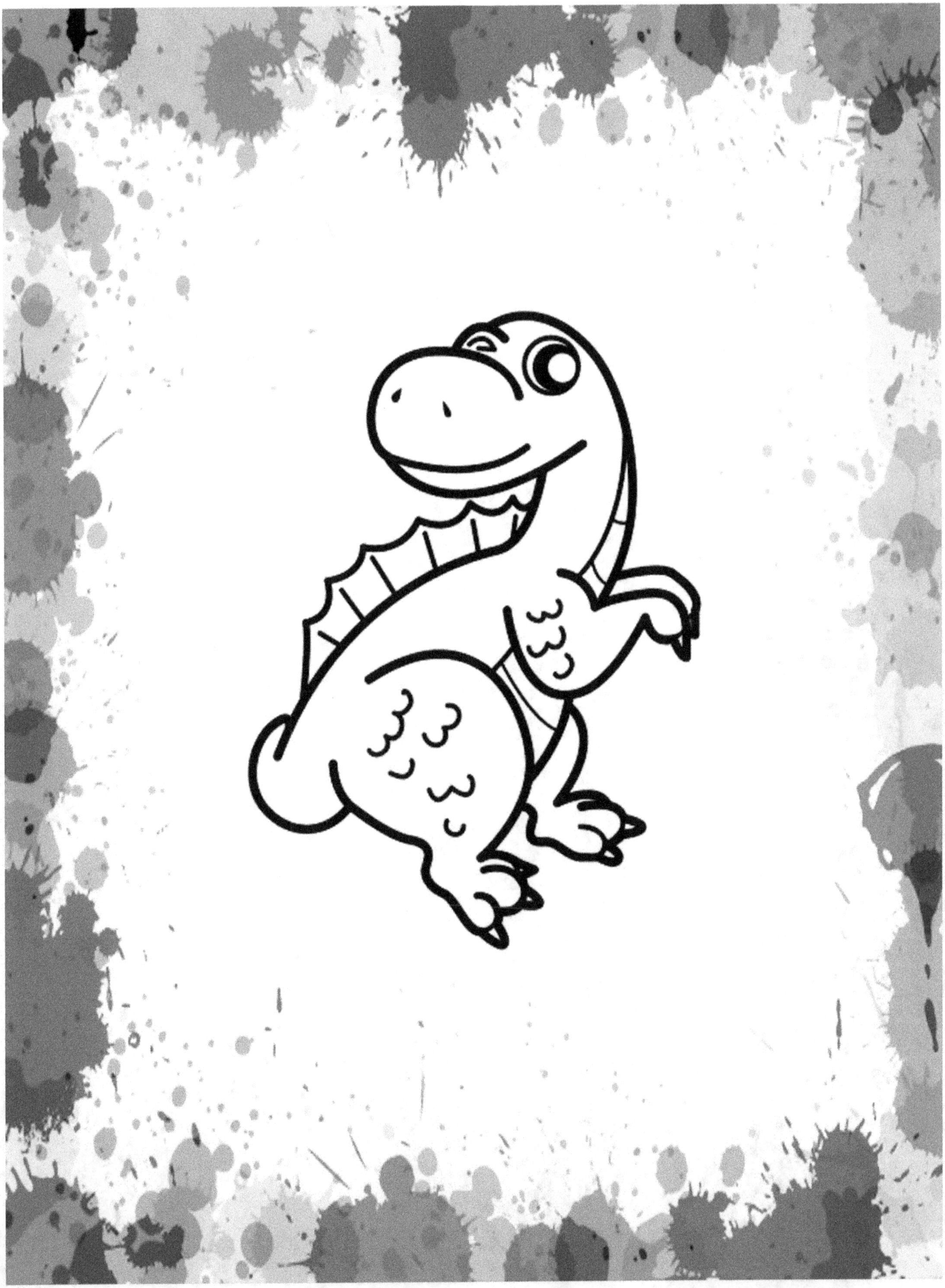

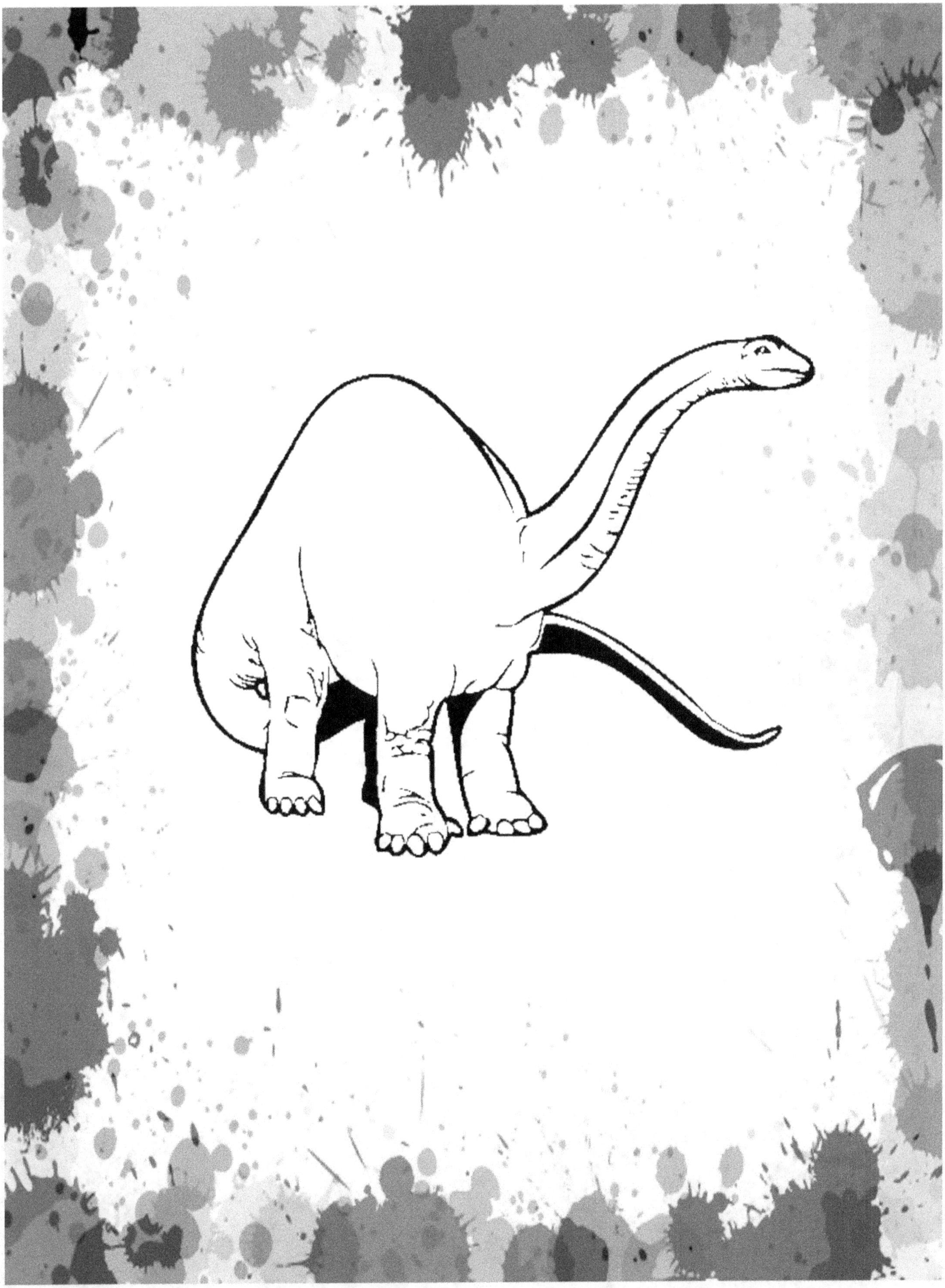

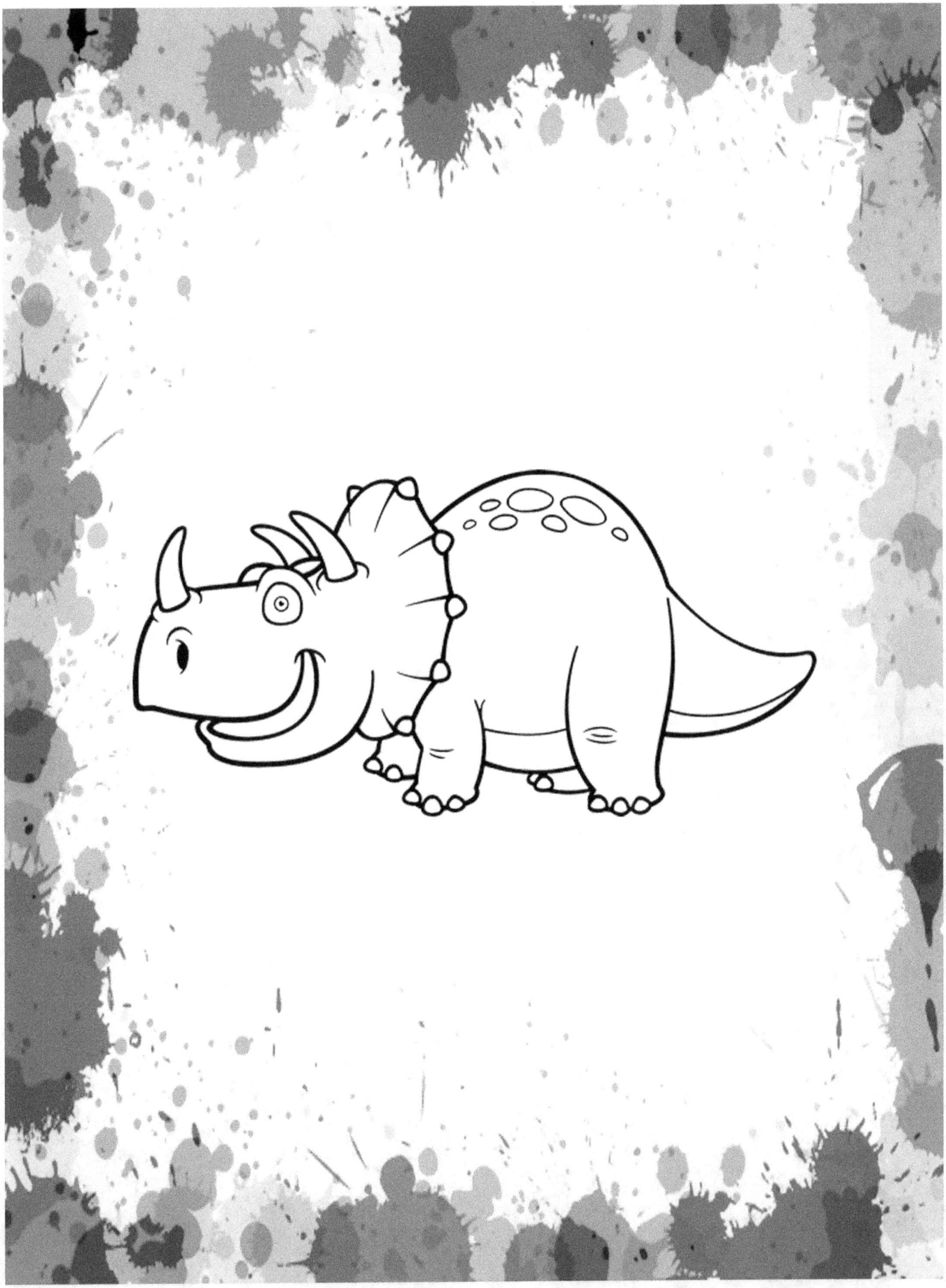

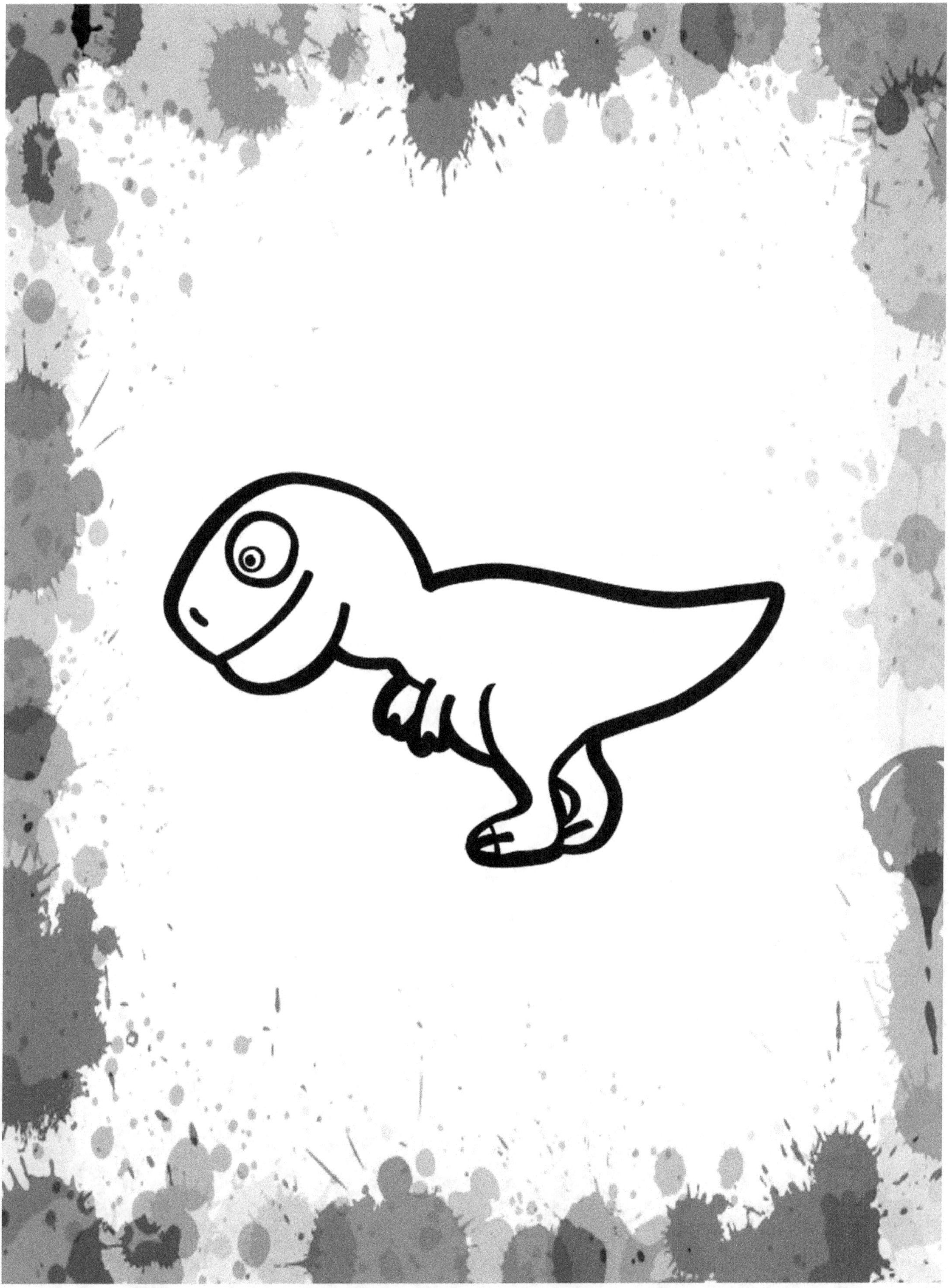

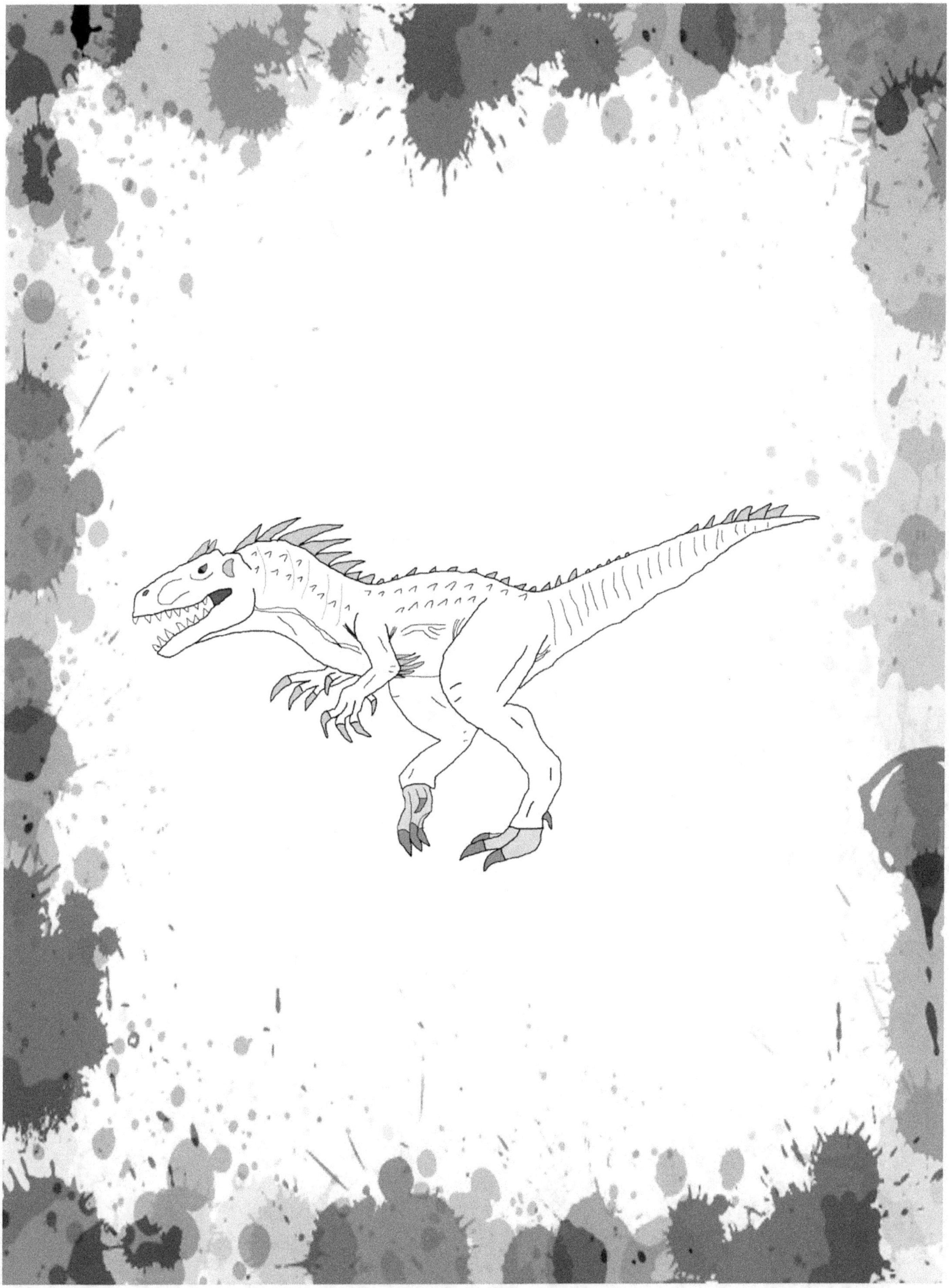

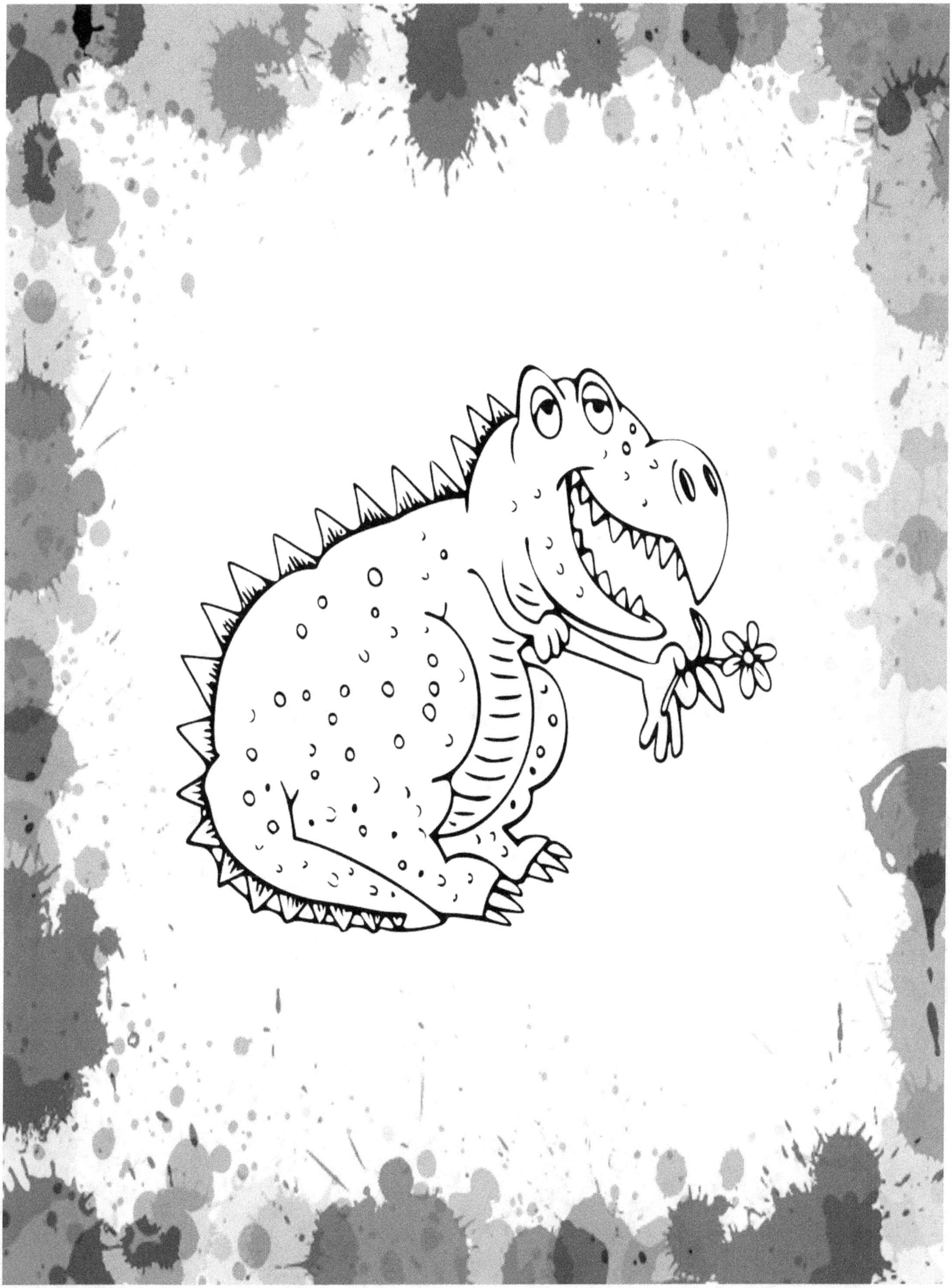

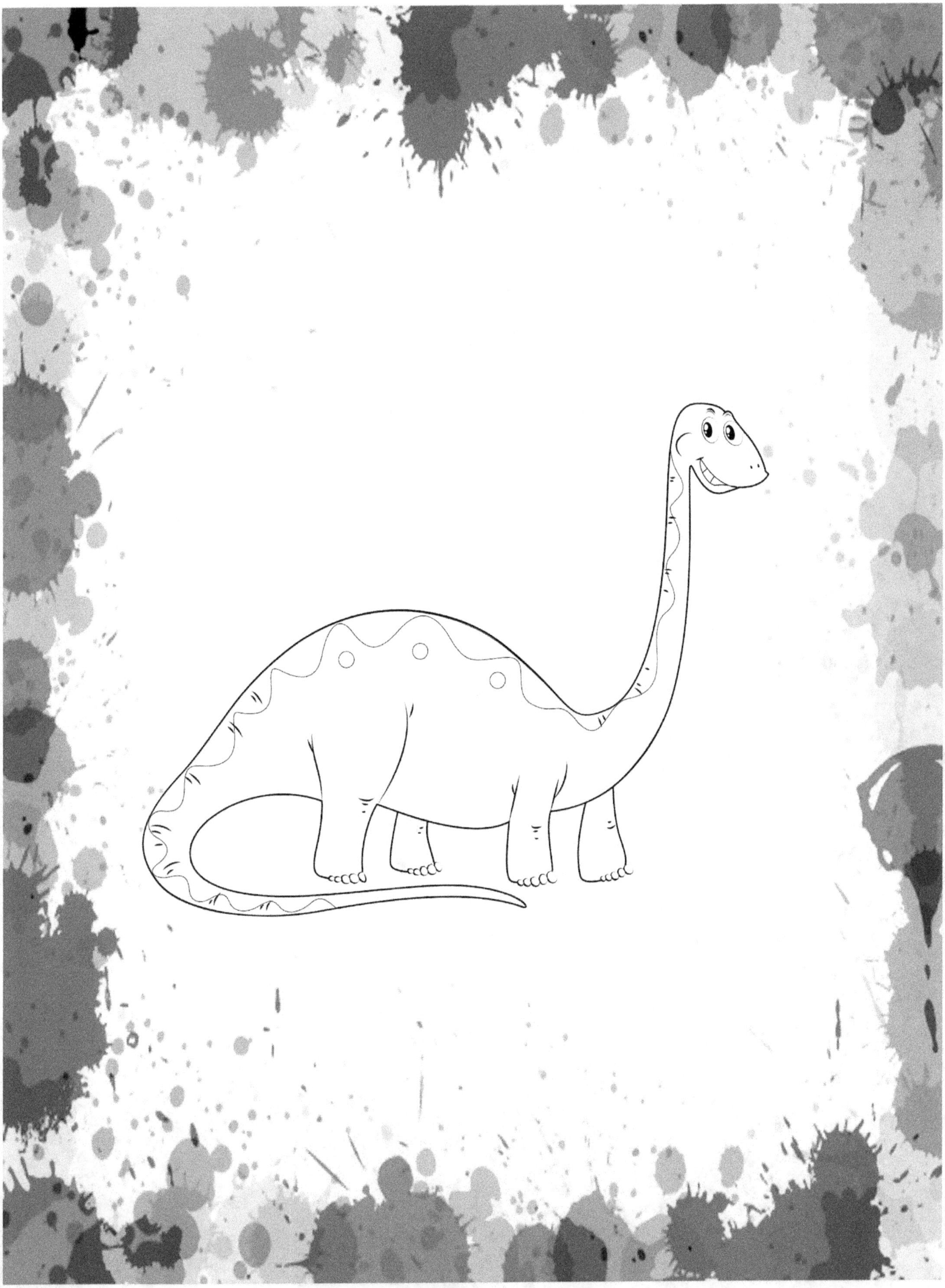

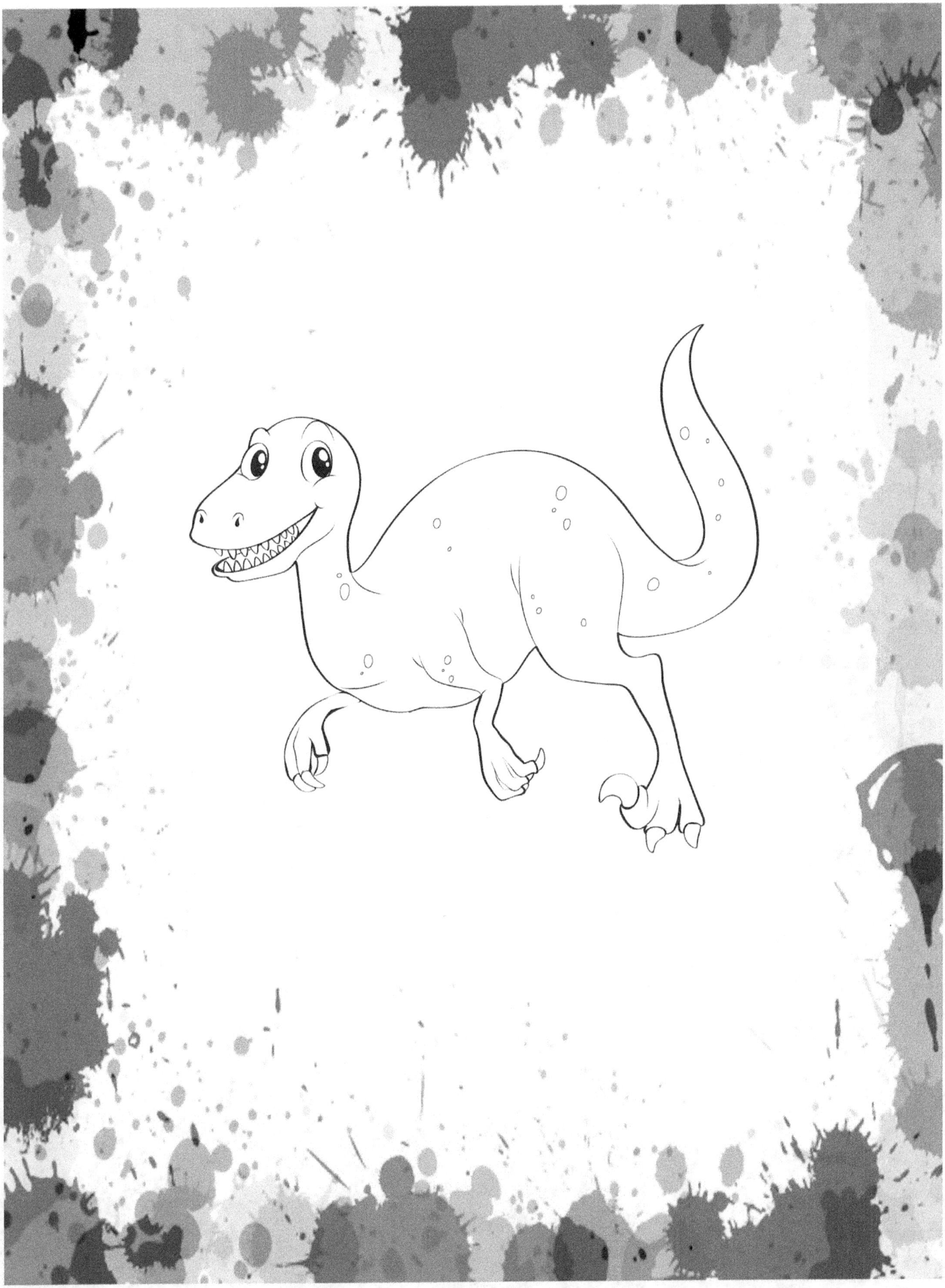

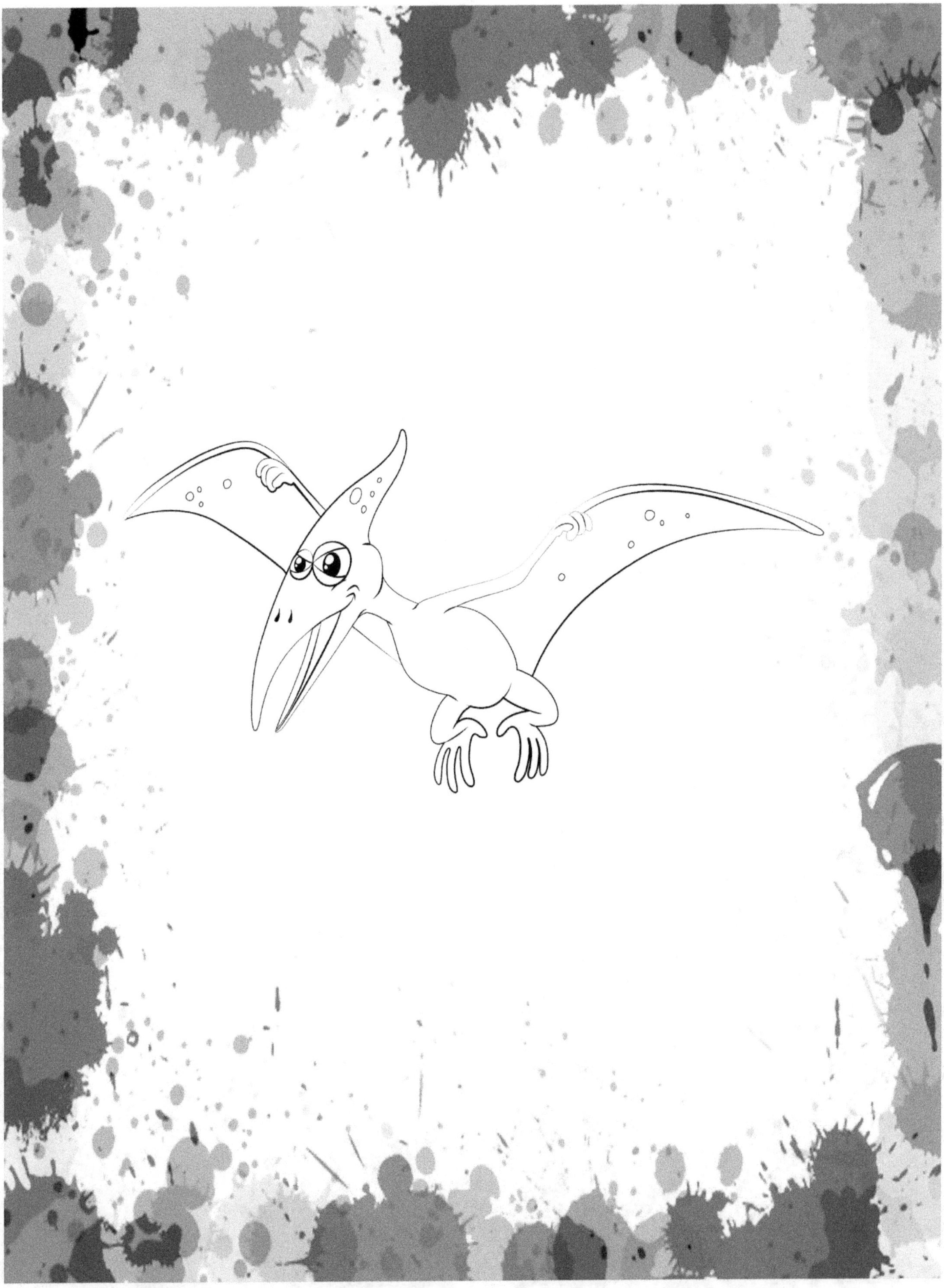

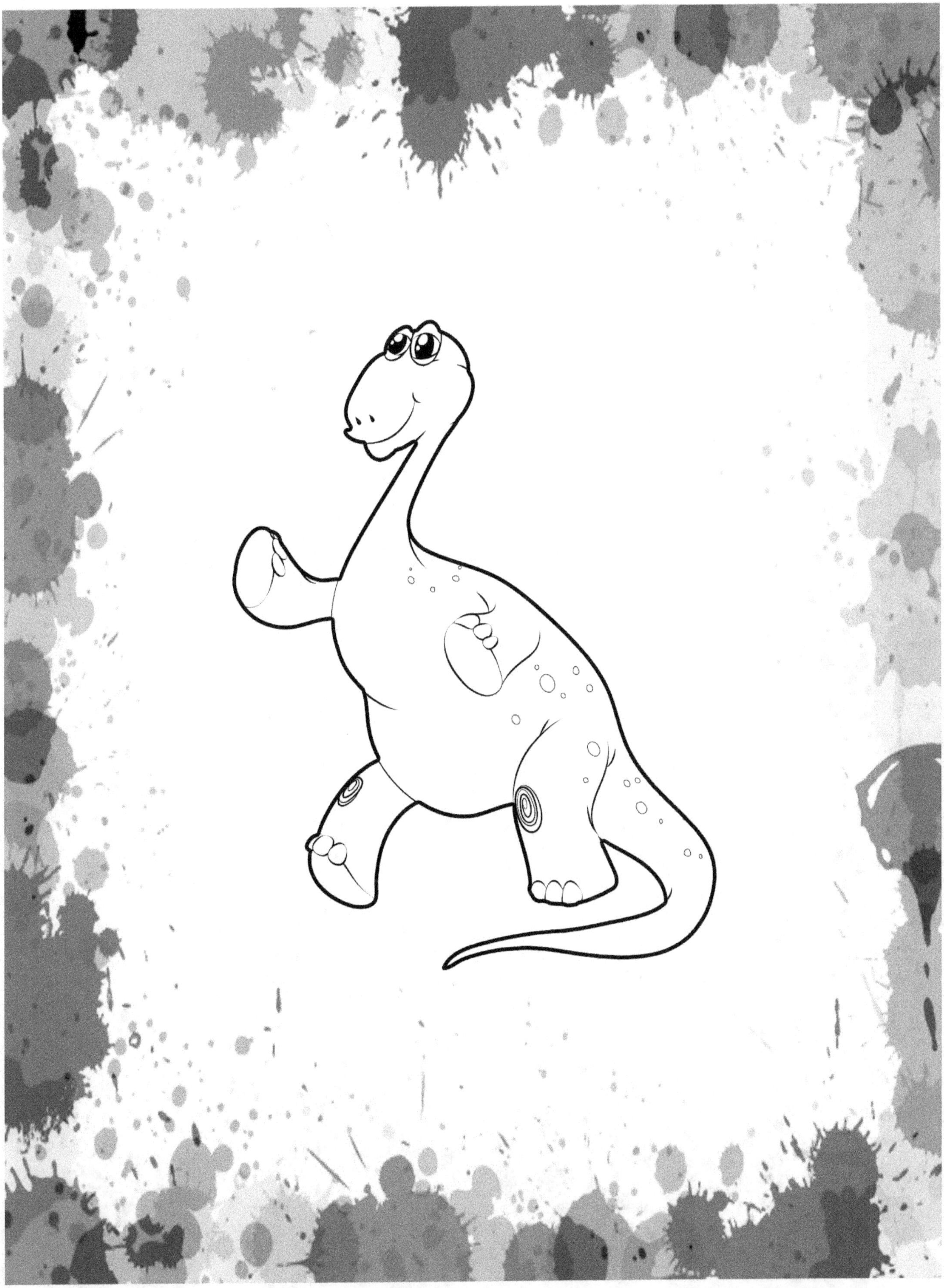

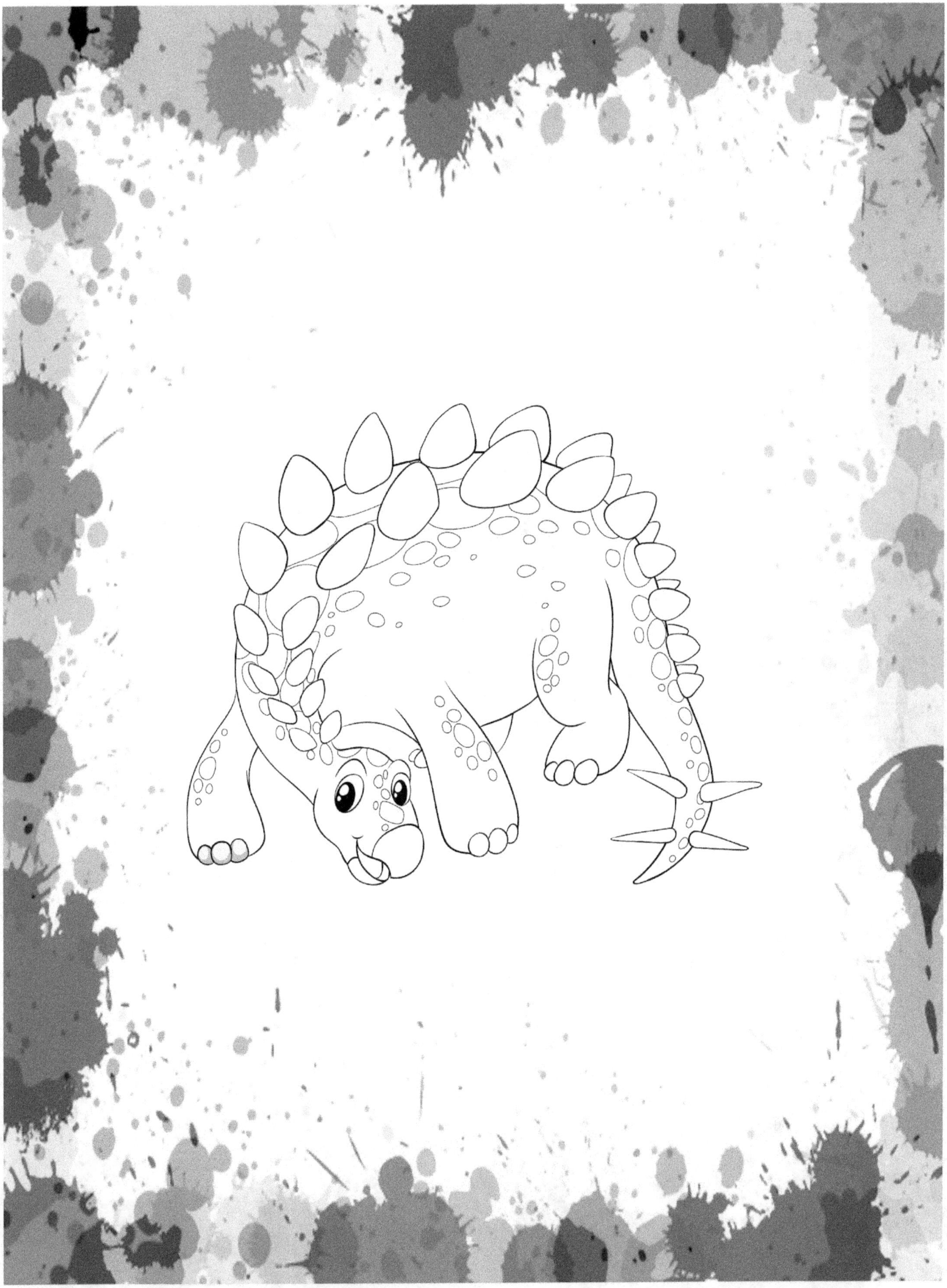

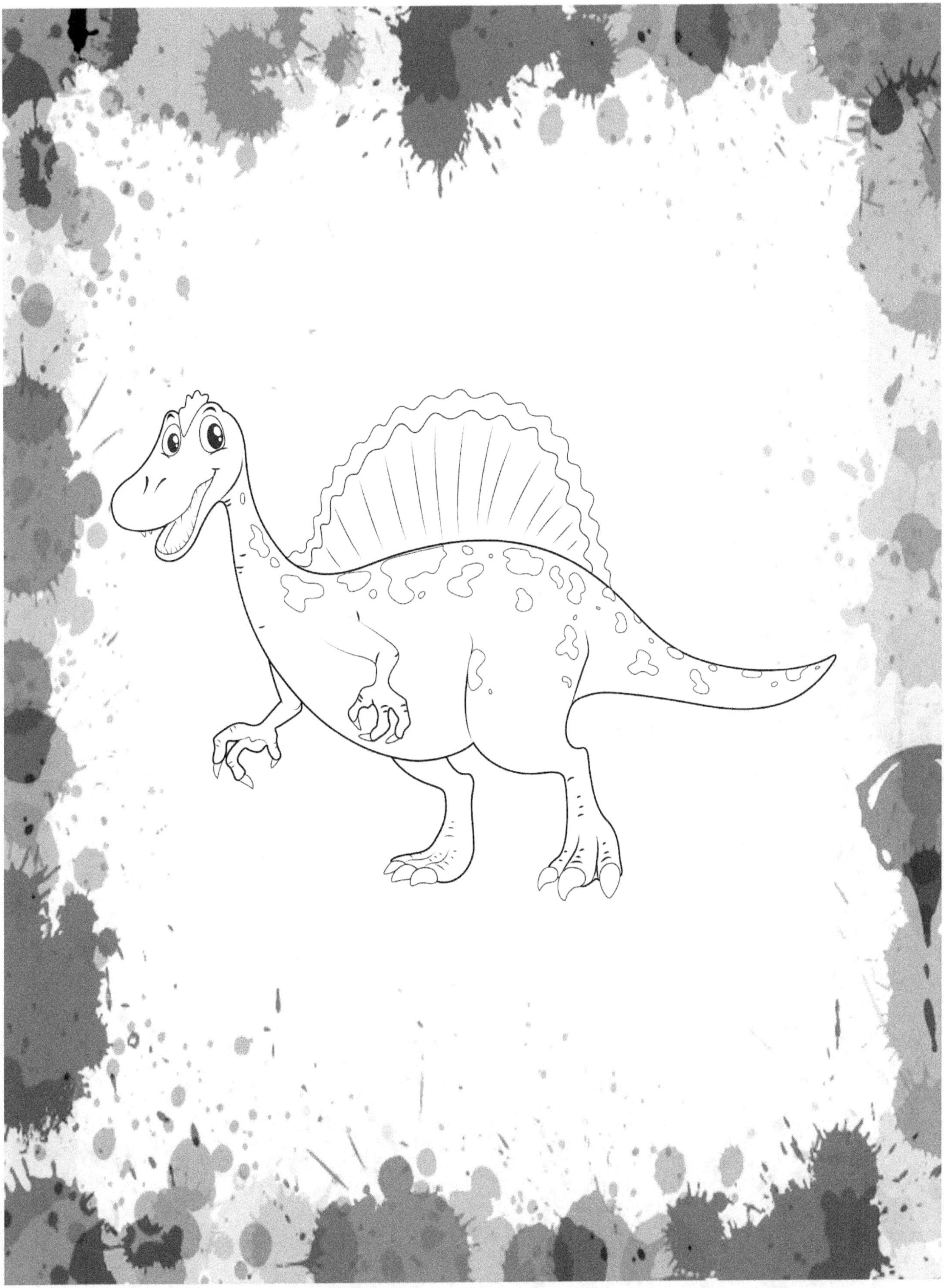

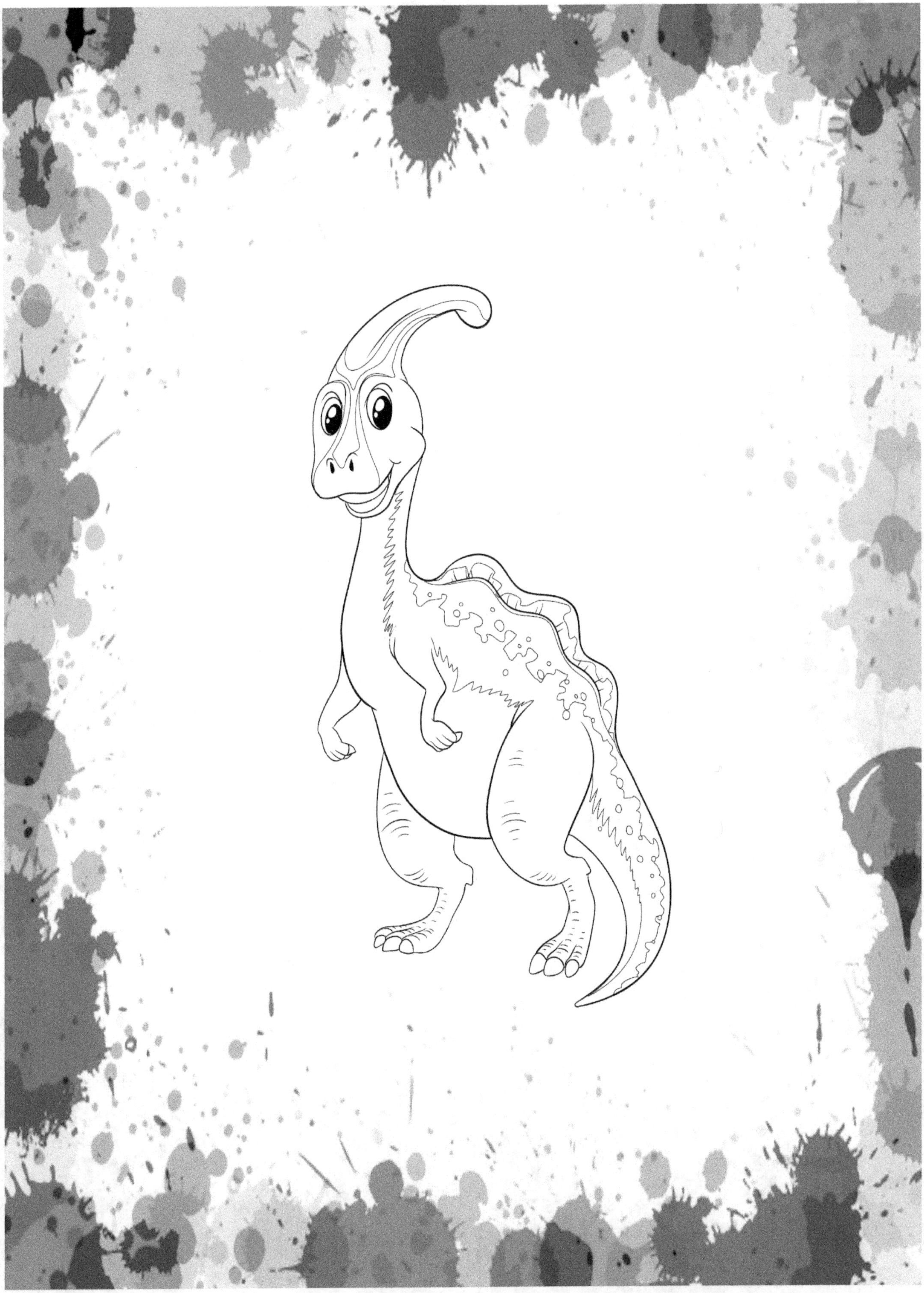

www.ingramcontent.com/pod-product-compliance
Lightning Source LLC
Chambersburg PA
CBHW080624220526
45467CB00011B/3353
9798683855369